FINDING YOUR VOICE IN A WORLD THAT NEEDS IT

Karen L. Gilliam, PhD

Finding Your Voice in a World that Needs It
by Karen L. Gilliam, PhD

Printed in the United States of America

ISBN 9781613798409

www.xulonpress.com

ACKNOWLEDGMENTS

My personal stories are interwoven with the various roles (female, African-American/ Black, wife, mother, grandmother, sister, council woman) where I claim membership. These experiences and the many people I've met along the way have influenced who I am. To my husband, his soft-spoken and patient companionship is like water to fish. I don't know where I would be without him in my life. It is a constant source of peace and security in my sometimes chaotic world. To my children, Carlo, Bianca and Danielle, your humor, perseverance and gracious heart have taught me well and I treasure the relationships we share. To Jim Stuart, whose kindness and generosity reached out to me, touching a stranger in a time of great need. To my sister, Michelle, whose amazing strength of character encouraged me throughout this writing journey. There are many who have had a part in shaping things I do — Mommie, Daddy, Debbie, Adrianne, Kay, Toni, Laura, Lena, Racine, Peggy, Mia, Bobo, Ann, Claude, Phil, Lonnie, Laurien, John, Carolyn. My life is so much richer because of you. And, I am indebted to you all. In no order of priority, I have borrowed from the writings of Jerome Bruner, Dr. John C. Maxwell, Parker Palmer, Lisa Nichols (The Secret), Dawna Markova and in other instances gained clarity from personal exchanges with Joan Southgate (Restore Cleveland Hope, Inc.), Barry Heermann (Noble Purpose©), and Constance Haqq (Reiki Master, Empowerment Facilitator). Collectively, they give meaning to "I am because we are." Their contributions speak to whatever qualities the book may possess; its flaws and omissions are all my own.

FOR THE LITTLE WOMEN IN MY LIFE

who inspire and love me unconditionally:

Karah

and

Reina

Table of Contents

Introduction

I can't imagine a single day without story, whether that story is a poem, the narrative of my first granddaughter's birth, the anecdotes and reporting (some true and some untrue) during my first political run for office, the pleasant or painful memories that emerge from watching a movie or reading a book, the saga behind a tragic accident or the account of walking the path of the underground-railroad.

Stories are a great way to convey important messages and teach lessons. While my mother was upstairs visiting with a neighbor, my brothers

"TELL ME A FACT
AND I'LL LEARN.
TELL ME A TRUTH
AND I'LL BELIEVE.
BUT TELL ME A
STORY AND IT WILL
LIVE IN MY HEART

and I were being mischievous in the basement. We started playing with the washing machine — not today's modern-day appliance with push buttons and memory chips — by putting our fingers close to the rolling pin that would grab and squeeze the water out of clothes. We took turns to see who was quick and the greater risk taker. Never questioning the sanity of choice or consequence, it was great fun and I never saw it coming. My fingers, my hand were suddenly caught! I was trapped and being pulled unwillingly by a monstrosity that would not let go.

So, too, do today's unpredictable and life-altering turn of events — in our world, community, neighborhood, workplace and in our families and relationships – seem to catch us, sometimes without warning, at what feels like the most inopportune time to deal with unwanted change and challenge. With so many commitments — to family, community, church, and work — I found myself stretched too thin and pulled into far too many directions. In this climate of uncertainty – escalating unemployment, tough economy, doing more and getting by with less -, like you, I am sometimes overwhelmed by the magnitude of it all. But most troubling, in all this busyness, was the realization that I was not showing up on my own list of priorities. By the time I completed all tasks for "you" and "them", there was no time for "I" and "me". Just as that old washing machine grabbed my attention and wouldn't release my hand, I had reached a point in life where Sonya Friedman's, a psychologist and former CNN program host, claim would not let go: "You have the greatest chance of being happy when the voice you respond to is your own voice".

Where have I been the happiest? Who was I with? What was I doing? What makes my heart sing with gladness? Have I been mostly thinking, speaking, writing and observing that which pleases me or not? What is it that I feel is lacking or missing? Can I even name it? There are facets of life that are fundamental to human fulfillment. Stephen Covey describes these universal dimensions as to live, to learn, to love, and to leave a legacy. The need to live is our physical need for such things as food, clothing, shelter, economic well-being, health. The need to learn is our mental need to develop and to grow. The need to love is our social need to relate to other people, to belong, to love, to be loved. And the need to leave a legacy is our spiritual need to have a sense of meaning, purpose, personal congruence, and contribution. We create our lives by the stories we tell day in and day out. What story am I telling myself and what story has yet to be given voice?

Finding your voice is not the destination; it is a manner of traveling. There are three essentials to pack before setting off on this voyage: *Sankofa*, Story and Questions. I invite you to take this journey on finding, trusting and using your voice in a world that needs it; for no one else can dance your dance, sing your song or write your story. *May Grace Be With You, Karen*

About This Book

In this book, I share a few stories of impactful memories surrounding my soul's search for meaning. Not in any deliberate sense, I seemed to have traveled along the four universal dimensions of life, discovering and re-discovering my sense of self. I find immense comfort in the healing power of stories. In remembering and reflecting on the peaks and valleys of my life and those of my ancestors and elders, I'm reminded to not live to regret what I didn't learn, love or try. Ultimately, this book is about the journey within to find one's voice while trusting that your path is as it should be.

Sankofa

Making sense of the world and my place in it cannot be left in the hands of others. Acknowledging the sense of one's past, present, and future is a true sign of self-awareness. We each must make our own journey and sometimes when you feel that you just can't go on, you may need to go back. I resonated with the pictorial symbolism in the writing system known as Adinkra, which was created by the Ashanti craftsmen of Ghana, West Africa. The Adinkra symbolize the Akan way of life, and individually each symbol can be associated with a proverb rooted in the Akan experience.

From *Sankofa*, a word derived from the words SAN (return), KO (go), FA (look, seek and take), the message is clear. It is not taboo to go back and fetch it when you forget or don't know. The mythical *Sankofa* bird has its feet firmly planted forward, but its head turned backwards, with an egg held tightly in its mouth. Whatever we have lost, forgotten, forgone or been stripped of, can be reclaimed, revived, preserved and perpetuated. Not only is there wisdom in learning from the past to guide future planning but we should reach back and gather the best of what our past has to teach us, so that we can achieve our full potential as we move forward. The Akans believe that there must be movement and new learning as time passes, but as this forward journey proceeds the knowledge must never be forgotten. The egg in the bird's mouth represents this knowledge of the past upon which wisdom is based and signifies the generation to come that would benefit from that wisdom.

The egg must not be held too tightly or it will break; nor too loosely or it will fall. The journey you take in finding your own voice influences every aspect of your life – spiritual, business, professional, and personal – and of those lives you meet along the way. Be careful of the wisdom that comes out of tradition, becoming so deeply rooted that you cannot move forward. Be thankful for the seeds planted for they brought you to where you are. Know that you are blessed, that you are loved and that you are here for some divine purpose. Start walking in your anointing. Be fully present in the moment. Look to a tomorrow that is full of promises for what is yet to come. Determine what you truly care about; then devote yourself to the pursuit.

Story

IT'S NEVER TOO LATE TO BEGIN LIVING THE REST OF YOUR LIFE.

I was introduced to *Sankofa* through story. Not just any story, but the tale of Joan Evelyn Southgate, who at the age of 73, traveled on foot, 519 miles of the Underground Railroad (UGRR), across Ohio, Pennsylvania, New York and into Canada. As noted in her book, *In their path: A grandmother's*

519-mile underground railroad walk (2004), it was from an ancestor's whisper that she was told to walk in order to praise the amazing people who walked hundreds and hundreds of miles running to freedom. Meeting people, and sharing stories, Ms. Southgate wove a narrative, connecting people across their differences, enabling the exchange of ideas and sharing of identities and sparking significant change in individual and collective behavior. Her story greatly influenced, what for me has become, a never-ending journey in finding and living one's signature purpose.

When I met Joan, I experienced a sense of well-being from the sound of her voice. It was as if she had reached into my restless spirit and discovered the lingering questions that stemmed from my own disconnection with family and ancestral history. Her story fed my soul. We talked about these brave African Americans who risked so much for freedom and her mission to heal the wounds of slavery. While listening to her storytelling, I felt a connection to my past that I had never been able to acknowledge before. I was reminded that rather than discounting or ignoring my heritage, it was important to recognize and reclaim its richness, its boldness and its bravery. So much of my familial past has been lost with the passing of each elder. But I still yearn to know from whence I came and how it has influenced who I am today. My desire to find and to trust my voice in proudly proclaiming my Black identity, and then to support others in finding voice and becoming all they were meant to be has become the fulcrum of my journey.

Questions

So much of what we learn and come to understand is dependent upon the 'right' question. I participated in a training program on an intentional change process. The facilitator introduced a concept and model, called 'immunity to change' that was developed and written by Robert Kegan and Lisa

Laskow Lahey. Their book by the same name helps participants better understand their competing commitments and truly understand the motivation behind behavior and why change, with all of the best intentions, can be so difficult to master. I tried to work through the mapping process but was stuck. Weeks later I was no closer to revealing the hidden commitments and assumptions that were blocking my progress, when the facilitator suggested that perhaps I was not working on the 'right' question. I offer this story to illustrate the sacred space that questions hold of being in the place between not knowing and your desire to know.

Life has given each of us questions that we can only answer for ourselves. Sometimes a question is just that — an expression of inquiry that invites or calls for a reply, an invitation to take that inward journey. Though I enjoy introspection and take pleasure in rich thought-provoking discourse with good friends, I sometimes struggle with the lingering of unanswered, sometimes unasked, questions or where one question simply begets another and yet another. Why me, oh Lord? When will this pass? Is this all there is? Sometimes His answer is yes; no; yes but later and [I'm sure] 'are you kidding?" My saving grace is *faith* in a loving God who wants to make things crystal clear, in spite of the fact that we keep asking until we get the answer we want or don't recognize that perhaps we're asking the wrong question. Philippians 4:6-7.

There are moments when the question is more important than the answer. Sometimes one right question asked at the right time can change the direction of your life. A few years ago while attending a formal dinner, I had the pleasure of being seated next to George Fraser, author and popular motivational speaker. After an engaging conversation, he paused to write a note on the back of his business card; handed it to me and asked that I think about it. "What gift(s) are you holding HOSTAGE from our community because of your personal fears!? I still have that card and on occasion will reflect on it because it is *my* persistent question. The questions in this book are meant to touch your heart and soul and to cause you to think about what is central to your inner core. Their purpose is to be the catalyst for the deep reflection needed on this journey of finding voice.

Sankofa, story, and questions serve as the framework for this book. Following each chapter story is a list of essential questions that elude simple answers. They are meant to probe into the universal dimensions of living, learning, loving and leaving a legacy, which are at the heart of the search for truth. The questions may prompt more questions and invite an even deeper reflection on your life and your world. This is my invitation to you – to take that inner journey to become clearer, more focused on creating the conditions for leading a purposeful life and to begin writing the next chapter of your story. This book is as much for me as I hope it will mean for your own search for wholeness. Taken from a sign on the front of the New York Ethical Society's building,

I invite you to turn the page and "Have your answers questioned here."

What Will I Answer?

Life has given me questions that only I can answer.

What difference will I have made by being here?
Will my voice be that of optimism and cheer?

Will I take what I've learned and pass it on
to the next?
Will my zest for living and loving never be at rest?

Will my voice speak for the voiceless,
the powerless, the few?
Will I have been a role model and shown how-to?

Life has given me questions that only I can answer.

Will I exercise my voice for truth and reason?
Will I become more of who I am with
each succeeding season?

Will I have carried as I climbed?

Will my tithe be in treasure or perhaps in time?

Will my voice respect the inner teacher?

Will beautifully sung songs be one of its features?

Will I have fought a good and just fight?

Will I *be* the answer that comes to light?

Life has given me questions that only I can answer.

What will I answer?

klmg

ON LIVING

ON LIVING

I know this now. Every man gives his life for what he believes. Every woman gives her life for what she believes. Sometimes people believe in little or nothing, yet they give their lives to that little or nothing. One life is all we have and we live it as we believe in living it. And then it is gone. But to sacrifice what you are and live without belief, that's more terrible than dying. – reportedly expressed by Joan of Arc

What are you willing to risk?

My husband and I took the opportunity to walk a simulated underground railroad.

We arrived early to check in and discovered that the assembled crowd was the 7:00 p.m. group. So we went back to the coziness of our car, anxiously awaiting our start time of 7:30 p.m. I noticed that there were very few people of color in the gathering. I didn't stop to question why I was looking for them. The wait wasn't too long before we set off on our hike. Our only light was from lanterns held by our three or four guides. We were led by one very tall and forceful-speaking man who demanded that we turn all cell phones off or put them on vibrate. "You are runaway slaves and called cargo. On this journey, we're never sure who is truly supportive or just trying to recapture runaways. The code words as we pass from one conductor to the next are: I'm a friend of a friend. The code name for Cleveland is Hope. The code name for Canada is Caanan. When the slave catchers are in the area we'll say that the wind is blowing from the South. When you hear that, run for cover. Keep close together and stay quiet. Are there any questions?"

There were none and so our journey began. At first, my husband and I simply walked side by side in silence. My eyes were focused on whoever happened to be walking in front or right beside me. The entire group was silent. If there were whispers, I couldn't hear them. I was aware of the stillness in the night air, the clearness of the sky as we gazed upward looking for the North star, the chill of both the season and the unfamiliar, our environs, the sound of our feet upon the ground and the periodic train whistle somewhere off in the distance. Freedom seekers learned how to tell direction from reading the stars in the night sky. Tonight would have been a good night for keeping on track. The stars were as bright as diamonds. Along the way, we stopped, not so much for a rest, but to

31

listen to vignettes re-enacted by volunteer actors. At our first stop and at the conclusion of the walk, we were asked the same question: "Could you do it? Could you leave all that you hate – the bondage and the cruelty - and all that you love – your family, your children, your home – to seek freedom?"

We walked. We ran. We cowered in the brush and shrubbery of wooded areas, hoping to remain hidden from the slave catchers' eyes. I was cold so clung tighter (for warmth and support) to my husband's hand. As the walk progressed, my body warmed, but only to be replaced with the discomfort of hunger pains. I was tired and my legs ached from bending, stooping low to the ground for cover, and the pacing of the walk. How much longer, I wondered. An abolitionist farmer hid us in his barn. But we were caught and put on a train headed back South.

Maya Angelou is quoted as saying: People will forget what you said. People will forget what you did. But they will never forget how you made them feel. I knew that I wouldn't remember everything an actor said. Nor would I have exact recall on every step of this walk. And though the feelings will be long remembered, I wanted and did capture my immediate reflections and feelings on audiotape once we were back and settled in the warmth of our car. I remembered the code names and password. But my most poignant memory is when we were captured in the barn and forced to come outside. "I want all you bucks over here and wenches over here," screamed the slave catcher. I was forced to let go of my husband's hand, to move away from him. "Keep your eyes to the ground. Don't look at me." How heartrending to be torn from a loved one. The slave catchers' voices grew louder and angrier. I wanted to look up to search for my husband. But to do so, I'd risk having their fury directed towards me. "Get the shackles and leg irons. Line 'em up. Looks like we got some twofers in the bunch." Silently we fell into a single line and with heads bowed down walked in the direction of the train. We were caught and being returned down South.

Moments later my husband caught up with me. I hesitated – were the slave catchers watching – before grabbing his hand. We boarded the train. It's over, I thought. "Sit down!" screamed the slave catcher. I immediately took a seat, surprised by my own quick reaction to the demand. "Wanna know how close you came to freedom? You was 27 miles." I could only imagine how a twofer might feel, having tried to escape twice and come so near to Cleveland, to Hope, to freedom, only to be re-captured and returned to bondage.

Reflections: There are, at least, three reasons why we need to remember the history of slavery, as told by Joan Southgate. First, as abolitionists and sympathizers, would we have been willing to break federal law to assist freedom seekers? In other words, with a similar or equally disparate challenge of today, requiring risk and/or sacrifice, would we have found our voice and be willing to exercise it? This is the question that must be answered individually and an answer that anyone who would want to lead needs to know. Second, slave owners portrayed African Americans as incapable of caring for themselves or organizing for the good of the community. The Underground Railroad refutes this claim as people from all walks of life assisted the freedom seekers and came together on issues of mutual concern. It's a lesson that should not be lost on today's challenges, whether they are of local, global, national or international affairs. For we as a people have the talent, the passion and the conscience to do what is right in creating our desired futures. Third, and I was reminded of this while writing this book, there was a time in history when many of my ancestors had no voice. Context is everything. In parts of our world today, there are conditions where people have little to no freedom of choice. But I am an American, living in the United States of America. Who or what is preventing me from articulating my voice? Am I my own roadblock? These are questions that anyone who wants to live and lead a life of purpose must ponder.

Questions on Living

The questions that follow are meant to evoke the purpose and passion (or lack their of) that are always

"THE FIRST PRINCIPLE OF SUCCESS IS DESIRE . . . DESIRE IS THE PLANTING OF YOUR SEED".
Robert Collier

in our intuitive minds. These questions are not asking what is the meaning of life, but rather asking you to consider and to define what your life and living means, realizing that we have a choice about the stories we tell and the stories we create.

Where are you willing to risk (and at what cost to) your significance?

Living is about making choices and taking responsibility. What does your life say about your choices?

What choices are you willing to make to redirect (the condition, manner and means of) your life and living?

Do you have a sense of self? Can you name what you are here for?

To move forward, you must reclaim the past. What is yours and yours alone to claim?

Where do you take a stand and who are you to take a stand?

Where do your talents and the needs of the world intersect (livelihood)?

We should reach back and gather the best of what our past has to teach us, so that we can achieve our full potential as we move forward. What are you willing to let go of that's getting in your way?

Are you still long enough to hear the whispers of your ancestors? What are they telling you?

What would it take to have the best year ever?

The questions for self-reflection on living, learning, loving and leaving a legacy are not mutually exclusive.

ON LEARNING

ON LEARNING

"Our deepest fear is not that we are inadequate. Our deepest fear is that we are powerful beyond measure. It is our light, not our darkness that most frightens us. We ask ourselves, Who am I to be brilliant, gorgeous, talented, fabulous? Actually, who are you *not* to be? You are a child of God. Your playing small does not serve the world. There is nothing enlightened about shrinking so that other people won't feel insecure around you. We are all meant to shine, as children do. We were born to make manifest the glory of God that is within us. It's not just in some of us; it's in everyone. And as we let our own light shine, we unconsciously give other people permission to do the same. As we are liberated from our own fear, our presence automatically liberates others." *A Return to Love* by Marianne Williamson

What do you fear?

My higher-education journey took twenty-five years, starting with an associate's degree in 1981 to obtaining a doctoral degree in 2006. Admittedly, my earlier love of learning was motivated by competition and competence. By the time I started doctoral studies any external drivers had been superseded by a constant curiosity and an intense yearning for the simple joys of discovering knowledge and understanding. But accumulating knowledge is only one aspect of learning. Experience is an equally compelling teacher.

I first became interested in the field of workforce diversity in 1989 during my MBA program. Little did I realize that far beyond an intellectual pursuit, this area of work would also be a stimulus for spiritual and emotional growth. With the support of the CEO at my place of employment, I started a diversity initiative that promulgated into wide-scale organizational change. In the beginning, as every good mystery story starts, I didn't know what I didn't know - about the emerging field of workforce diversity and the requisite skills and abilities to be an effective change agent in managing the work and leading a team in this endeavor. One of the most difficult situations that people face is dealing effectively with inappropriate, offensive humor. I am no exception. It is one thing to provide guidelines and to tell others how to best respond. But being put to the test is quite another matter. It's where the rubber meets the road; where the devil will try to destroy your purpose.

I had relocated within the organization to another geographic location. Within a few weeks, I was asked to be one of a group of facilitators at a week-long management development retreat. I was thrilled by the opportunity to showcase my skills and to further network with other managers. One evening, a small group of maybe eight individuals had gathered for friendly banter after a long and intense day, when one of the more senior participants used his positional power to take over the conversation for purposes of telling a joke. It is only important, for contextual reasons, to note that I was the only Black female in the group. As if being called to attention by the master sergeant, when this powerful figure interrupted the conversation, everyone's voice fell silent. His storytelling seemed harmless until what I heard next sent shockwaves to my system. I couldn't believe my ears. Derogatory and dehumanizing, the 'N' word spewed out of his mouth. It was hurtful. I sat stunned in disbelief and embarrassment. How dare he use that word in my presence? What was he thinking? Am I of such little consequence? How could he? As my body started to feel warm and my heart to beat faster, I felt the danger. I didn't need a mirror to know that my ears were probably beet red. I was angry. Every offensive word I'd ever learned was swimming around in my head as I mentally reached the busy intersection of Stop, Go or Proceed with Caution.

This was my first major assignment upon relocating to a new area of the country. He, the offender, was a powerful employee, capable of ruining my career. I either believed in all that I advocated or was parading around as an imposter, leading only when the calculated risk was small. I'm no saint; nor did I believe in that critical moment that the offender deserved my respect. Yet, if I were to proceed it was more important to provide a safe container for the conversation that needed to occur. Simply put, I had to walk my talk. I took a deep breath, exhaled, and began talking to him in a quiet, measured tone of voice. One person tried to intercede by placing his hand on my arm and explaining that he, the offender, didn't mean anything by it. In turn, I placed my hand on the arm of this would-be mediator and in a respectful manner responded: "This is a conversation between him [the offender] and me." The silence was deadening in the room. It was hard to breathe but I managed to force the air into my lungs and continue. "Why would you use such a word? Why wouldn't you think that I'd find it personally offensive?" "I didn't use it," said the offender; "it was only part of the story I was telling. Someone else used it. I was merely repeating the story". Again, I asked: "Why would you use such a word? Didn't it occur to you that I'd be offended? Though his eyes met mine, he seemed to look through me, never really seeing me. Moments later he stood up and quietly left the room.

The reactions were varied. A few apologized for laughing, explaining that it was their only way to release the embarrassment. One stated that he simply froze, not knowing what to do or say. Another hugged me and remarked that she was glad that I had spoken up because no one had ever before dared to confront the offender's widely-known, except to me, disrespectful behavior.

 Sometimes in the learning, we teach; sometimes in the teaching, we learn. Was I – in this shared experience - a student or a teacher? My colleagues were left with questions of their own, questions that left them uneasy and not fully answered by any other. I had experienced a teachable moment.

Reflections: In Matthew's sermon on the mount, he tells his disciples: "Neither do men light a candle, and put it under a bushel, but on a candlestick and it giveth light unto all that are in the house" (Matthew:4:15). On this particular night, in 1995, the Lord revealed my purpose in what was only a ten minute encounter that felt like an eternity. "Let your light so shine before men, that they may see your good works, and glorify your Father which is in heaven" (4:16). My emotions had not held me prisoner and placed a stronghold on my voice. I conquered a fear; stepped out on faith and into that vulnerable space; and passed a personal test that left my integrity intact. Finding your voice is a beginning. Finding the courage to use your voice, so as not to block your spiritual gift, is a life-long journey. There is no outer conflict that does not have an inner conflict. In that moment, however, I could not have known which came first — learning that I was worth standing up for or finding the courage to take a stand on something greater than myself. I was strengthened as a human being, as a Black woman, as a leader, for having taken a stand for something that I believed in – the dignity and worth of all human life, including that of my own.

Questions on Learning

This journey of learning, knowing, and mastering your self does not require you to become something greater than you are. It merely requires absolute fidelity to your own authentic path.

What do you love more than you fear?

"WHAT YOU DO SPEAKS SO LOUDLY THAT I CANNOT HEAR WHAT YOU SAY."
Ralph Waldo Emerson

What is unfinished for you to learn?

What are you curious about?

What is unfinished for you to experience?

What learning opportunities are presented by your shadow, your blind spot, or the baggage you carry around?

Are you stuck in your own story? Are you willing to let go of an unproductive story?

Are you still long enough to hear the whispers of your own voice?

What from your past will help you achieve your full potential in moving forward?

What are the conversations you're having with yourself? Are the stories you tell yourself self-defeating, getting in the way or uplifting and carrying you forward?

What have you learned about your strengths? How are you applying your strengths to your passion?

How are you nurturing your gifts and talents?

Are you learning what you need to learn? How do you know what you don't know?

What have you ignored, not accepted and/or forgotten?

Do you pay attention to physical, mental, and emotional experiences of the moment? What do they tell you?

Are you willing to close the gap between what you know and what you need to know?

Do you allow others to discover what they need to learn?

Are you open to new experiences, new ideas and different meanings and interpretations?

The questions for self-reflection on living, learning, loving and leaving a legacy are not mutually exclusive.

ON LOVING

ON LOVING

Living teaches us that loving matters. It is when we are most vulnerable or suffering from the pain of loss, disappointment and disconnection that we realize just how much it matters. While we can create stories that will help us actively engage with and care for each other, we must also tend to our own needs to be fully awake and alive.

What are you willing to let go?

I was leading a divided life. My career, to this point, had been quite rewarding.

The longest I had worked for any one organization was about 10 years. Each move was deliberate in terms of career advancement, greater levels of responsibility, along with professional growth at a commensurate salary. So when I was approached by a trusted colleague to interview for what I saw as a "dream" position, I completed my pros and cons analysis before leaving a good company where I was a well-respected member of the senior team. The first year on a new job is what some refer to as a honeymoon period. I was learning the culture, the politics, the people and the job, and building relationships. About eighteen months into the position and after countless incidents, I recognized, more accurately was forced to acknowledge, that the dream had become a nightmare, spilling over into my personal and family life.

It was distressing, difficult and painful to show up at work. Even within the seclusion of my own thoughts, I could not describe the events of a day without crying. Day after day, following sleepless nights, I'd return with a hope that my prayers would be answered. The story I told myself was: "You're smart; figure out how to make it work. You deserve to be here. You earned it. Don't be weak. You've survived worse. Mommie died at the age of forty-five. You thought you couldn't go on. Your baby brother was murdered at the age of twenty-five. Life was unbearable. Your eighteen year old nephew, along with three other young people and a toddler, lost his life in a tragic car accident. You were crushed but endured it all. For God's sake …this is, after all, just a job. Besides, you have a responsibility to your family. And then perhaps in a nobler stance, my ego cried out 'You have a responsibility to your staff, to your internal clients. You do good work and they need you.' This job is part of your career strategy." And so, being a perfectionist and workaholic and while holding on to this false self-image of a miracle worker, I swallowed my tongue and put on a good façade.

But it was to no avail. I wonder how many times we try the same solution before learning that it's crazy to think if we keep doing the same thing, we'll get different results. I was physically and emotionally spent, drowning in a sea of misery, when I lost my voice, literally. I really didn't see it coming, the proverbial straw that broke the camel's back, but it hit me in a fit of uncontrollable crying. I was like a dam that after years of holding back the waters, collapsed under the weight and force of unexpressed pain. I lost my voice, spiritually. In *Sankofa* terms, I had been holding the egg too tightly and it finally broke.

I questioned how could this happen to me? Why did this happen to me? I felt betrayed. A circle of trust had been broken. I was angry, hurt, and floundering in an altogether unfamiliar terrain of not being in control of my emotions. Like Humpty Dumpty, "threescore men and threescore more, could not place Humpty as he was before." But I did not want to go back to what I had become — a stranger to myself.

Parker Palmer, author of *A hidden wholeness: The journey toward an undivided life* (2004), best captures my state of being when he said: "…I was living my outer life at great remove from my inner truth. I was not merely on the wrong path, I was killing my self-hood with every step I took." How did I come to this? I was at a total loss for any rational explanation that I could cling to.

I have friends who send me wonderful email messages. Sometimes a prayer, a cartoon, or simple words of wisdom arrive at just the right time. One day, I opened an email to read:

At twenty, we worry about what others think of us;

At forty we don't care about what others think of us;

At sixty we discover they haven't been thinking about us at all.

Others and they. What about what I think? And, therein lies the problem. I don't know whether it was an unwillingness or an inability, but I never took the time to give thought to what I was allowing to occur in my life. To the outside world, I appeared to be living the good life. The changes – loss of appetite and zest for life and taking daily refuge in my home office or bedroom - were noticeable only to my family. They didn't know how to help me and I didn't know how to help myself.

Over the ensuing months [and after leaving this environment], I found the courage to tackle a relentless question. Why had I remained in a setting that steadily killed my spirit? The facts were: I valued the security of a high-paying salary and the social standing of my position over loving my true self. I worried about what others – family, friends, and significant strangers – thought and completely dismissed what the universe was telling me. Where I once believed that holding on at all costs makes one stronger, I now know that sometimes it's in the letting go. Today, the why me question is more easily answered. My path – the ups and downs, the pain and the joy - is as it should be. I had to learn, in the only way I could, what it means to deeply care about myself. I am divided no more.

Reflections: You may find it odd that this story finds its way "On Loving" pages, but it is a story about love — that is, self-love. Palmer identified other forms of the divided life: We refuse to invest ourselves in our work, diminishing its quality and distancing ourselves from those it is meant to serve.

- We make our living at jobs that violate our basic values, even when survival does not absolutely demand it
- We remain in settings or relationships that steadily kill off our spirits.
- We harbor secrets to achieve personal gain at the expense of other people.
- We hide our beliefs from those who disagree with us to avoid conflict, challenge, and change.

• We conceal our true identities for fear of being criticized, shunned, or attacked.

Professional career women, of all shapes, sizes and colors, find themselves bearing hardships and carrying burdens for many. They give moral support to their family and friends, bringing joy, hope, love, and compassion to those whose path they may cross. But, they – we - forget our own worth and neglect to care for ourselves. "Let all bitterness, and wrath, and anger, and clamor, and evil speaking, be put away from you, with all malice; And be ye kind one to another, tenderhearted, forgiving one another, even as God for Christ's sake hath forgiven you" (Ephesians 4:31-32). These two scriptures capture the essence of my story. The lack of forgiveness will keep our prayers from going up. Holding on to heartache only prolongs the pain. Let it go. Be kind to yourself, love yourself and above all, forgive yourself.

Questions on Loving

The source for many of these questions come from a diversity of thought leaders and cover self-love, spiritual love, love of avocation, and love of others.

What's stopping you from becoming who you were meant to be?

> **"I AM SPECIAL BECAUSE I HAVE LOTS OF CRAYONS."**
>
> Karah (my seven-year old grand-daughter)

What are you doing for self-care?

What are you doing to maintain your energy, to support your greatness?

What do you like/love about your identity?

What's hard or painful about your identity? Is it something that you can change? Is it something that you want to change?

Are you doing what you love and loving what you do?

Can you name what it is that you love?

What is precious to you? What speaks to you, touches you, or turns you on?

Where is your passion? For whom or for what do you hold that passion?

Whether in your local neighborhood, your community-at-large, your church or business environment, how do you come to this work?

Does this path have heart?

What helps you sustain your work? What gets in the way of sustaining your work?

Giving out of a deep sense of love energizes you. What do you love more than you fear? How can you motivate yourself by what you love?

What have you done to bring the gifts of those on the periphery into the center?

When was the last time you acknowledged that others make a difference?

What do you love about yourself? Be specific.

What do you like/love about your identity?

How do you celebrate your greatness?

How are you involved in the project of your own life?

The questions for self-reflection on living, learning, loving and leaving a legacy are not mutually exclusive.

ON LEAVING A LEGACY

ON LEAVING A LEGACY

In one sense leaving a legacy is about money or property bequeathed to another by will. It also bears fruit as an intangible gift passed on to others, a way of paying it forward. "Somewhere out there is a unique place for you to help others — a unique life role for you to fill that only you can fill." (Thomas Kinkade)

Will I have done my best?

At a monthly morning meeting of Cleveland Coach Federation, we were led through

a series of exercises in pairs or groups of three where we took turns finishing the statement: "Who I am is ..." My initial responses started off with the roles I play in life. Who I am is a mother. Who I am is a grandmother. Who I am is a wife. Who I am is a sister. Who I am is a daughter. We were timed so this first round was easy. Then as I listened to others I began to see parts of myself in their responses. Once it was my turn again, I started. Who I am is an OD practitioner. Who I am is a coach. Who I am is a council woman. Silence followed as I pondered on what I would say next. Time was up. It was someone else's turn. On the third iteration and only after I had exhausted the familial and societal roles did I consider characteristics, qualities and character. Who I am is a trusted friend. Who I am is a good listener. Who I am is a work in progress. In this exercise, the third time was the charm before I started to think at a deeper level on what it means to be me.

On my life's journey, it was when I became a grandmother that I started to think deeply about what it means to leave a legacy. Yes, I enjoy accolades. It feels good to be included on a who's who list. But there's a longing that says there must be more for me to be. For if I'm not a parent, who am I? If I am not a manager, who am I? If I am not a councilwoman, who am I? And so on. In the end, how do I want to be remembered? While I'm living, loving and learning, what is waiting behind the door to make its entrance? On thoughts of legacy, among my first inclinations is to reflect on famous people. With the 2008 election of our 44th president of the United States, Barack Obama, I was reminded of a verse now seen on collectible t-shirts, mugs and other memorabilia from the historic election of the first African American/ black president:

Rosa sat so Martin could walk

Martin walked so Barack could run

Barack ran so our children could fly.

Rosa Parks, Rev. Dr. Martin Luther King Jr., Barack Hussein Obama are known throughout the world for the impact that their lives had and continue to have on others. Then I thought about our local she-roes. Lena Nance, age 68, was honored, along with 24 others, in the Older Volunteers Enrich American program. In 2008 she contributed 1,656 hours alone at a local hospital. Though retired, she is now among the escalating statistic of grandparents who have become the primary caretakers of grandchildren. Lena still finds time to give back to hundreds, maybe thousands of patients that cross her path. Joan Southgate, who turned 80 in 2009, completed the final leg of 219 miles of the UGRR walk on May 30, 2009. With each step, she literally continues to write her legacy. Her gift of grace is in helping others write and perhaps complete their own stories.

I sought a definition with which to continue my reflections. The American Heritage® Dictionary states that legacy is something handed down from an ancestor or a predecessor or from the past and/or it can be transmitted by or received from a significant stranger. Leaving a legacy for others to follow is not limited to the famous; the first to achieve a celebrated milestone; the extraordinary person; nor is it regulated to a certain age group. As I think about those who've left indelible marks upon my heart, they include many: parents, grandparents, uncles, teachers, friends, and colleagues. Not all of their gifts are of regal magnitude, nor do they need be. *Sankofa.* In 1 Timothy, Paul the Apostle advises Timothy on the personal conduct required in caring for the church and reminds him "neglect not the gift that is in thee, which was given thee by prophecy" (4:14). As Paul continues to reflect upon his own ministry in 2 Timothy, he urges Timothy to carry on the work, being mindful to "stir up the gift of God" (1:6) that is within him. The meaning I give to leaving a legacy is to do what I can, with what I have, where I am. I, too, want to know that I have used my gifts in a way that is pleasing to God and that "I have fought a good fight, I have finished my course, I have kept the faith" (4:7). Sometimes there's an immediate gratification to making a positive difference in someone's life.

At other times I'm planting a seed. And the amazing nuance of this affirmation is that I never know when or whether the seed has taken root.

My cohort [during doctoral studies] was comprised of nine adults who came from all across the United States and are diverse in age, profession, personalities, socio-economic and marital status, gender and other dimensions of diversity. Bill was a military pilot, is a successful entrepreneur and now an esteemed professor. He's about 6 feet in height, slightly grayed; a thinker who carefully chooses his words and has the likeness and personality of a big teddy bear. As we were preparing to leave from our first 3 ½ days of residency, I gave him a good-bye hug. With each subsequent residency, we learned more about one another, developed trusting relationships and started sharing heartfelt thoughts and private dreams. Bill confided to me that he had never been a hugger and was quite surprised by that first embrace. But now he looked forward to seeing me at every residency and getting his hug. Our cohort spent the next four plus years bonding as close to one another as any nucleus family. One day, post PhD studies, an email arrived announcing that Bill had suffered a heart attack and was in fair condition. One cohort member immediately was on track obtaining the details and status on Bill's condition. The good news is that Bill is doing extremely well and recovering nicely. Within a week's time, we received a personal note from him.

Hi to all cohort one. thank you all so much for your concern, prayers, support and love...especially the hugs Karen.

Last Monday I awoke at 4:00AM not able to catch my breath. Mollie (Bill's wife) took me to our Physician and she immediately sent me to Riverside Hospital in Columbus, which happens to have an excellent heart institute. After being admitted in the ER, I was observed for several hours and the decision was made to keep me overnight for observation. While in a room on the heart monitoring floor around 7:00PM, three nurses ran into my room. Thinking I wasn't so old after all Bruce (another cohort member), they asked if I was feeling well. I said I was a little tired and light headed but I thought I was well. One of the three, Kim, immediately called Code whatever and about a dozen people were swarming around me. The next thing I know the Doctor, not like us but an MD, said my heart had stopped. I knew he was correct because I told him yes, I am dying. I said that everyone was sounding like an echo and they were fading away and that the feeling was leaving my feet and legs. The Doctor whose name was Doctor Fu said that I was dead. It was so incredibly peaceful. I did not see the "white light" or faces of loved ones as some say, but rather just peaceful, lying there watching Doctor Fu yelling at everyone and people scrambling all around me. The next thing I remember was getting hit by what seemed like lighting... the paddles like you see in the movies...300 jewels. There was this loud explosion sound in my head and everything was completely black then the brightest white I had ever seen; then black again. I remember saying something like "&!@%!!" and everyone laughed at me. I was coming back to life and then they told me that they were going to intubate me, take me to the heart cath lab and three days later the breathing apparatus was removed and I woke up in ICU. They had implanted a pacemaker in my chest. Evidently, there is the plumbing side of the heart, which was not the issue with me. My arteries are relatively clear, which was determined while they were looking inside my heart. My issue is much more deadly in that the electrical rhythm of the heart failed and it just stopped beating. Three doctors told me that if I had not been in the hospital and if the "Crash Cart Team" had not responded so quickly and if Doctor Fu, the expert on such issues had not been on duty as opposed to a resident I would not be alive today. 95% of the people this happens to die and those are the ones in the hospital. The ones out of the hospital never make it. It seems that the stars were aligned. After 3 tours and 111 combat sorties in Vietnam and being shot at, chased by Migs and Sams it almost ended with a heart issue. This has been a life altering experience and I plan to relax more, not be a Dean anymore and just teach some graduate level classes. Thank you again to all of you and I love all of you like brothers and sisters. I hope Cohort One will always be a close family. Bill.

Did you catch the last four words of the salutation? I did. "...especially the hugs Karen." An indelible mark left on the heart. "Henceforth there is laid up for me a crown of righteousness, which the Lord, the righteous judge, shall give me at that day" (4:8). When He looks at my life, I want to stand before Him knowing that I've done my best as a daughter, mother, wife, grand-mother, sister, Christian, neighbor, and friend.

Reflections: This story holds rich dimensions of life. It is sure to conjure up thoughts on living, learning, loving and/or leaving a legacy. One might ponder the life altering experience of being close to death and being brought back to life. Or, the connectedness and love one feels from the touch, the gentleness, the kind word of another human being. No one can tell you how to find your purpose, your calling, your soul's code, your voice. But living your signature purpose on purpose is the gift you bequeath to others.

To whom does it matter? It must first matter to you. Meaning isn't something you find; it's some-thing you give. Give and it will be given to you. There are countless memories that tell me that I've made a difference. Examples abound with a daugh-ter's childhood friend who is grateful for the time I took to listen, a youth in a summer employment program who chased me down in a shopping mall to say thank you for caring, a resident in my ward that called to express appreciation for a small act of kindness, a family reunion trip with my granddaughters where the four year old turned to me one evening and said "you're the best mama in the whole world". Whether it's my time, talent, love and/or compassion, I have received considerably more in return. Our world needs for each of us to find our voice, to get our life on purpose and to bring our whole self forward. Your gift – your legacy – depends on it.

Questions on Leaving a Legacy

There is power of life and death in the tongue. Anyone can speak words that tend to rob another of the spirit to continue in difficult times. Special is the individual who speaks life to those who cross her path.

What's the one thing you could do now that would make the biggest difference? And for whom?

THE BEST TIME TO
PLANT A TREE IS
TWENTY YEARS
AGO. THE SECOND
BEST TIME IS NOW.
- Proverb

What do you care so deeply about that you're willing to step out on faith and act on that belief?

What do you hope for?

Have you identified where and how you can be most helpful in providing service to others?

What have you achieved? What do you want to achieve?

What have you come here to give?

What is made different because you were here?

How are you tending to future generations?

What do you want to create together that would make a difference?

Are you leaving a legacy that enables others to live bigger lives than you have?

What difference have you made by being here? What difference will you make by being here?

The questions for self-reflection on living, learning, loving and leaving a legacy are not mutually exclusive.

WHAT WILL I ANSWER?

WHAT WILL I ANSWER?

Sunset and Sunrise

As I thought about the stories that I chose to share with you, the reader, I realized that they symbolized both a sunset and sunrise. In some ways, they reflect significant moments in time; a surrender of some limiting beliefs that kept my voice at bay; and a learning, oft times a re-learning that happens each and every day when we pause to think about our personal histories. As there is no night without day, my stories are also symbolic of a sunrise; a time of new beginnings, complete with new opportunities and choices. In his thought-provoking book

"Crossing the unknown sea," David Whyte cautions that if we do not invigorate and re-imagine our work it can slowly starve our spirit. Have I become too complacent in the daily routine of the existence I've crafted for myself? What questions have I avoided answering? What is unfinished for me to learn and to do? What will I answer for those questions life has given only to me?

There are many ways to be involved in your community, with some roles more prominent than others. A great deal of my time during the past twenty years has been spent in some form working in the political arena. I can imagine as I reference "politics", you've already dashed up the ladder of inference, as popularized by Peter Senge (1994) in *The Fifth Discipline Fieldbook*. In the time it's taken for you to read the last sentence, you've perhaps reasoned, based on your beliefs, prior experience, assumptions and certainly the news media that all politicians are not to be trusted, believed or [fill-in-the-blank] with some other unflattering and disparaging conclusion.

This is a modern-day dilemma that I find disturbing and begrudgingly accept as a personal challenge that goes with the territory of being an elected public servant. At a recent church service, a guest speaker talked about his involvement with a new organizational initiative called *Purple America*. Their focus is on creating new forums to share beliefs, engaging young people in meaningful dialogue about values, and connecting all Americans through the discovery and celebration of our shared American ideals. This work resonates with my own inclination to working on behalf of younger generations. But what also grabbed my attention was his story about how he came to this particular organization. After an unsuccessful bid for political office, he decided that it was meant for him to work for the greater good *and not in politics* where, in his synopsis, the greater good could not be found. How distressing for any one of any age, but in particular for our young adult citizens, to believe that being in politics is incongruent with working for the greater good.

I am committed to living a political life that tells a different story. "Polis" is the Greek word for city, and the derivation of the word, "politics." For Aristotle the field that studied the supreme good for society was politics and as we learn to give voice to our vision in the context of a public act, we are engaged in the art of politics. I started as a street representative; then became an officer in our homeowner's organization. My name first appeared on a ballot with nine others when I was elected to serve on the 10-member charter review commission. I volunteered to speak at local clubs and organizations on behalf of a candidate for office, which ultimately led to serving as a co-chair for three different election campaigns. These were all wonderful, and for the most part fun, opportunities to be engaged in meaningful work.

But I was ill-prepared, when I stepped into the unknown frontier of running for a contested council seat. I was introduced to a wave of unpleasant, untrue statements made, both verbally and in print, about me

— all in the name of political campaigning. As sure as the sun rises after it sets the evening before, there is no consequence that is not preceded by choice. I knew that politics had an unattractive, even ugly side but I didn't know how it would feel to be the object of someone's public scorn. Sticks and stones may break one's bones but words can kill the spirit. The insults were hurtful and gave pause to question why anyone would want to run for a public office. But run I did. My advisors said: "You've got to toughen up. You have to let these things roll of your back." Because I was characterized as someone who had no opinion, no platform, and essentially no voice, I wrestled with menacing questions. Do I fight fire with fire? Should I focus on the negativity and ridicule my opponent? What was I willing to do in order to garner a vote? At what cost was I willing to risk an election? What did I love more than I feared? There are some conversations to which we should not descend; some roads that are not meant for us to travel; and some costs that would bankrupt the soul. And just as certain, there is no softer pillow upon which to lay one's head than that of a clear conscience. I found the courage to stand firm in my belief that it is not necessary to run a "dirty" campaign in order to win an election. I placed faith in my own voice and trusted that those listening would recognize the veracity and feel the congruency that would enable them to find their own truth. Voice can be expressed in multiple ways (speaking, writing, singing, acting) and that of voting. Early results showed that I had won by twelve votes. An automatic recount resulted in a successful bid for office by ten votes, albeit ten voices. As the *sun is setting* on my second term in office, I am stronger in my vision for doing all that I can to work on behalf of the young people in my community.

My goal is to ensure that we find ways to involve teen-agers in local government and to offer more programming and educational opportunities for leadership development. It is sometimes frustrating that change comes about so slowly. What I've learned from the daily experiences of council life is that you don't plant seeds on untilled soil. It took time and patience but I was successful in obtaining full council support in passing legislation to 1) include two resident teen-agers as members of the city's community life committee and 2) allow two teen-agers to attend the annual National League of Cities Conference. Much to my surprise, both efforts were reported in what was then our local newspaper, The Bedford Sun Banner, in June 2009 by Robert Nozar. The entire article follows.

"There are some ideas that are more difficult than others, as it relates to getting support for that idea. Some go over like lead balloons, while others take off and soar. It's the nature of proposals that are put forward, particularly those that are suggested by politicians who are looking for ways to better their communities. An idea that is definitely in the popular category is the one presented Monday night to the Bedford school board by the Bedford Heights City Council. The plan is for members of that City Council to take along a pair of students from their city when they travel in late November 2010 to Denver for the annual meeting of the National League of Cities. While this plan has the support of the Mayor and the entire City Council, make no mistake about it: This is an idea that was first brought up more than a year ago and has been carefully nurtured by Ward 4 Councilwoman Karen Gilliam.

The initial response Gilliam received from colleagues last year was positive, but even good ideas, those that are well received, would die for lack of attention. Gilliam was not about to let that happen. She kept pushing it and pushing it, and soon found more than nodding support from other council members. Council President Phil Saunders got behind the idea and so it was that the plan really began to take final shape in early spring in a most unlikely place — the clubhouse at Thistledown Race Track. The Democratic Club of Bedford Heights was having its annual gathering at the track, and much to Gilliam's pleasure many of the people who could help make her idea a reality were present. So it was that Gilliam lured then-Superintendent Marty Motsco to a secluded corner of the dining area, away from the Democratic revelers. She wanted to go over the details of her plan another time. Saunders joined them at a table where fancily folded napkins were pushed aside as Gilliam pointed out specific points on a pile of paper. "Where's Phil?" someone asked Councilwoman Wendy Grant, who was keeping an eye out to make sure everyone at the event was getting what they needed. "Don't bother him now, he and Dr. Gilliam are with Marty," Grant said. "They need her support if taking students to the 'League' meeting is going to become a reality." Viewed from a distance it was clear that Saunders and Gilliam had Motsco's rapt attention. They didn't even notice that the panoramic view offered through the huge clubhouse windows included the day's fourth race, an exciting event that wasn't decided until deep in the home stretch. This was not the first time that Gilliam has been an advocate for innovative ideas that enhanced the education possibilities for the children of Bedford Heights. She pushed for students to be made members of City Council's Community Life Committee's advisory group. Gilliam figured that since students were among the biggest users of the city's recreation options it only stood to reason that they should be among those offering ideas to city leaders. And so it was on Monday night that Gilliam took center stage to explain to the school board all about the idea to take two students to the National League of Cities gathering. There wasn't a doubting Thomas in the group, with the only cloud over the whole concept being the difficult economy and tightening budgets that could stifle a plan for anyone to attend the meeting, much less two students. But still, this was not a time for negativity. Because of Gilliam's (and her elected colleagues) persistence and determination, the belief is that the economy will strengthen and everyone can move forward in this unique and bold idea to better prepare this area's leaders of tomorrow. Whether it's fundraisers, donations from local businesses, or the financial support of average residents, there just has to be a way to gather the money necessary to make Gilliam's dream a reality. It's just too good of an idea to let it die."

Due to the economic decline across our country and the fiscal emergencies that all local governments face, we cannot budget for council to attend the National League of Cities conference which, in turn, affects our plans for taking youth delegates. As the *sun* sets, it also *rises*. Our newest member of council has given voice to empowering our young people and with full support of council has successfully started a Youth Scholarship Fund. With donations from residents, business and friends of the community, in 2011, the city of Bedford Heights was able to give three financial scholarships to graduating seniors who reside in Bedford Heights and have definitive plans to further their education. The seeds have taken root.

The Untilled Soil

In continuing with my story, I'll return to a few lines from David Whyte's poem, "What To Remember When Waking".

You are not

a troubled guest

on this earth,

you are not

an accident

amidst other accidents

you were invited

from another and greater

night

than the one

from which

you have just emerged.

He was born in St. Clairsville, in southeastern Ohio on April 30, 1930. The youngest of ten children, his siblings were all distinctive in their chosen careers, ranging from that of military service, politics, social services, and musical arts. After graduating from Indiana University, he joined the Army as a commissioned ROTC second lieutenant. On his way to becoming a full colonel, he served as a platoon leader and as a company battalion and brigade commander. He advanced to chief of plans for the Far East & Pacific Division in the Office of the Deputy Chief of Staff for Military Operations at the Pentagon. The retired Army colonel earned numerous decorations, including the Legion of Merit, a Bronze Star Medal for valor, another Bronze Star for meritorious service, the Meritorious Service Medal with Oak Leaf Cluster and the Air Medal. When he retired in 1976, he taught secondary mathematics for the Cleveland schools; was a director for a proprietary school, a human resources manager; and owner of two privately-held businesses. He remained actively involved in community affairs, as a trustee of Clean-Land, Ohio and volunteering with United Way. But the most memorable role for Milford "Mick" L.

Marshall was that of my friend, father and grandfather. When I think about my commitment to service, I don't have to wander far to understand how it was part of my DNA to serve.

"If your purpose is only about you, it has no branches. If it is only about the rest of the world, it has no roots." It seems that I've devoted myself to bettering the lives of others, whether it has been through an elected office, my professional career, or as the matriarchal figure to a growing family. But something is missing. *Sankofa*. To move forward, you must reclaim the past. Whatever we have lost, forgotten, forgone, or been stripped of, can be reclaimed, revived, preserved and perpetuated. When my grandmother died in 19xx, she took what I thought was the last remaining hope for re-connecting with my maternal ancestry. I have long questioned and hungered for more details about my grandmother's family — my family. Whenever we'd ask questions about her mother and father, she refused to answer and so I fill the unknown with morbid thoughts. What was so awful about my grandmother's early life that she refused to share any stories? My oldest daughter, Bianca, wonders about the connection of simple things. As a youngster, she would ask my pale complexioned grandmother: "What are you?" Waiting for a response of either Black, White or mixed race, my grandmother would say: "I'm purple with pink polka dots!" My six-year old grand-daughter, Reina, is bi-racial. Her favorite colors are pink and purple. A silly coincidence without meaning? I don't know. What is unfinished for me to learn and to do? I don't know what I don't know about this side of my family. So, I've decided to explore this untilled soil, to being the search in finding my roots and who knows what stories may emerge that will inform the present and further define my future.

A CONVERSATION GUIDE

W elcome to this conversation guide. No matter how you work with this book, its ultimate goal is to encourage you to find your voice in a world that needs it by inviting you to take that inner journey – to pause, to reflect, to reclaim your past, and to actively engage with your present in creating a desired future.

The Internal Conversation

Though by definition, a conversation is meant to be an oral exchange of sentiments, observations, opinions, or ideas between persons, I'm suggesting that you create the space and time for reflecting on your beliefs, thoughts, interpretations and conclusions; in essence thinking about your own thinking. How might you be suffocating your own voice? Our lives are informed by stories, those that are passed on from generation to generation and those of our own creation. They can teach, celebrate, affirm, as well as disempower and demean. "Once people claim their voices neither they nor the world will ever be the same again" (Grace, 1999). Each chapter in this book has a story and how I made meaning of that story. Yet, the power of story is that we can each take what we need from that narrative. We read or listen to a story, try it on, and ask what does it reveal? What came up for you as you read my story? What stories do you tell yourself? How do you know what you know? What story is waiting for your voice? The asking of a question can create change. At the end of each chapter story are questions for you to consider. What keeps reoccurring for you? In the stillness of your mind, what thoughts are pressing and won't leave you alone? What are the crossroads facing you in your life or work? What questions has life given you to answer?

Certain books, movies, quotes, music, and art can deepen your thinking. The references in this book represent readings that resonated with me. Has anyone provided you with a quote that had great meaning to you? Some movies are incredible doorways to our essence, revealing new pathways to meaning and purpose. What lyrics and/or soundtracks of various music genres conjure up old hurts or pleasant memories? Immersing yourself in the quiet solitude of art or nature is an equally rewarding experience. So, I ask: What might it be like to take time for yourself, to find quiet moments in nature, to spend peaceful time alone or with others, to sit by a campfire or listen to the creek, to nap underneath a tree, to write or draw, or to enjoy the simple luxury of slowing down and doing absolutely nothing? How might your life be different if you allow your soul to wander?

Individual and Group Work

While on this journey of personal discovery, I participated in several (face to face and via teleworkshops) Noble Purpose© gatherings. *Noble Purpose* is both a book and a process, developed by Barry Heermann, Ph.D., that through guided conversation, meditation and facilitated exercises opens the space for accessing your purpose. I re-learned the value of solitude and became re-acquainted with journaling. Our process included the ritual of keeping a gratitude journal using the concept of "grateful for some / grateful for more." *Sankofa.* To return to my essential self, I must go back to what I have forgotten. I know that I am a child of God. But when in crises, I sometimes forget what I know to be true. "He maketh me to lie down in green pastures: he leadeth me beside the still waters. He restored my soul" (Psalm 23:2-3). To get in touch with my own significance, I must create space within myself which then allows me to create space with and for others.

The Conversation Circle

Don't limit your possibilities for renewing and connecting to your true nature. Anything that I've suggested for individual work can be applied in a circle of unity. As women, we know how to relationally attend to our families, our work, our community and all the external demands of being a daughter, wife, mother, grandmother, sister, aunt and friend. Within all of these roles and heart connections it is also important to find a sense of your inner being, your ground, your strength and connection with the sacredness of everyday life.

I have found that fertile ground with a special group of women, where we can sit together, talk about what's important to us and simply be. My noble purpose - to support and build community with people who believe in something greater than themselves and to help others clarify their signature purpose – has found a voice in this conversation circle.

We are seven women who come together with purpose to support one another in identifying strengths, expanding horizons, and finding voice. Our gatherings are diverse, sometimes over a communal meal in the comfort of someone's home, a visit to a museum, a jazz show, a play or intimate sharing during a weekend retreat. I am beholden to these women and have learned to not take for granted the simple pleasure of trusted conversation. During a facilitated "Empowerment" workshop session, I was asked to reflect deeply on my core beliefs, as well as any deep hurts that I had not let go. The beliefs were not difficult to surface: for example, that men will disappoint you (as taught by my grandmother), that as a Black female I must be twice as good as any other non-minority candidate (as taught by my elders and experienced early in my career) and that I am all alone, in the sense of not having a trusted confident to talk with. One of my dearest friends, Debbie, lives in California but was home for the Christmas holiday. We've been friends since 5th grade, so invariably after a long absence from seeing one another our conversation travels back to our disagreement over a 5th grade spelling bee contest and the teacher's pet. We can and do talk about anything – from hairstyle, to old loves, to impending retirement years. Her ability to listen deeply and without judgment is a gift to me. As I talked about her, a great sadness overcame me. I miss her. I miss us. With my voice cracking and the tears starting to flow, I had to let go of a false belief. I can miss my dear friend, while acknowledging and accepting the specialness of my conversation circle. And so, I thank these ladies for providing that sacred space, a circle of trust, where the soul is welcomed, the spirit uplifted, and sometimes hurts healed. I am because we are encircled in a rare form of community.

BIBLIOGRAPHY

Bridges, W. (2004). Transitions: Making sense of life's changes. Cambridge, MA: Da Capo Press.

Covey, S.R. (2004). The 8th habit: From effectiveness to greatness. New York, NY: Free Press.

Featherstone, J. (1989). To make the spirit whole. Harvard Educational Review, 59, 367-378.

Grace, B. (1999). Ethical leadership: In pursuit of the common good. Ethical Leadership Monograph Series / 1. The Center for Ethical Leadership. Seattle, Washington.

Heermann, B. (2004). Noble purpose: Igniting extraordinary passion for life and work. QSU Publishing Co.

Kouzes, J.M. & Posner, B.Z. (1999). Encouraging the heart: A leader's guide to rewarding and recognizing others. San Francisco, CA: Jossey-Bass Inc.

Marci. (2007). A grateful path: Inspirational thoughts on unconditional love, acceptance, and Positive living. Boulder, CO: Blue Mountain Arts, Inc.

Markova, D. (2000). I will not die an unlived life: Reclaiming purpose and passion. Boston, MA: Red Wheel/Weiser, LLC.

Palmer, P. J. (2004). A hidden wholeness: The journey toward an undivided life. San Francisco, CA: Jossey-Bass.

Senge, P., Kleiner, A., Roberts, C., Ross, R., Smith, B. (1994). The fifth discipline fieldbook. New York, NY: Doubleday Dell Publishing Group, Inc. Crown Business.

Southgate, J.E. & Stewart, F. (2004). In their path: A grandmother's 519-mile underground railroad walk. Solon, OH: Eagle Creek Press.

Whyte, D. (2001). Crossing the unknown sea: Work as a pilgrimage of identity. New York, NY: Riverhead Books.

CPSIA information can be obtained at www.ICGtesting.com
Printed in the USA
270028BV00001B/3/P